Hello, Sunshine!

Hello, Sunshine!

WITH ILLUSTRATIONS BY

BETSEY CLARK

Charming

and Delightful Proverbs

to Warm the Heart

Selected by Barbara Kunz Loots

♔

HALLMARK CROWN EDITIONS

Hello, Sunshine!

A heart full of thankfulness,

A thimbleful of care;

A soul of simple hopefulness,

An early morning prayer.

Build a little fence of trust
Around today;
Fill the space with loving work
And therein stay.

Betsey Clark

When we sigh about our trouble,

It grows double every day;

When we laugh about our trouble,

It's a bubble blown away.

A cheerful heart
and smiling face
Pour sunshine
in the darkest place.

The world is so full
of a number of things
I'm sure we should all
be as happy
as kings.

Joy will dance
the whole world through,
But it must
begin with you.

Oh, the joy and comfort
You through life may know,
With a song of sunshine
Everywhere you go!

You have to believe
in happiness,
It isn't an outward thing;
The spring
never makes the song, I guess,
As much as the song
makes the spring.

Oh, better than the minting
Of a gold-crowned king
Is the safe-kept memory
Of a lovely thing.

When you wish
for something new,
Believe it's on its way
to you...

...And when the time is right,
you'll find
You'll have just what
you had in mind!

A laugh is just like music,
It lingers in the heart,
And where its melody is heard,
The ills of life depart.

A house is built of logs and stone,
Of tiles and posts and piers;
A home is built of loving deeds
That stand a thousand years.

Anger in its place

May assume a kind of grace,

If it has some reason in it

And never lasts

beyond a minute.

God bless,
when winds blow,
Our home
and all we know.

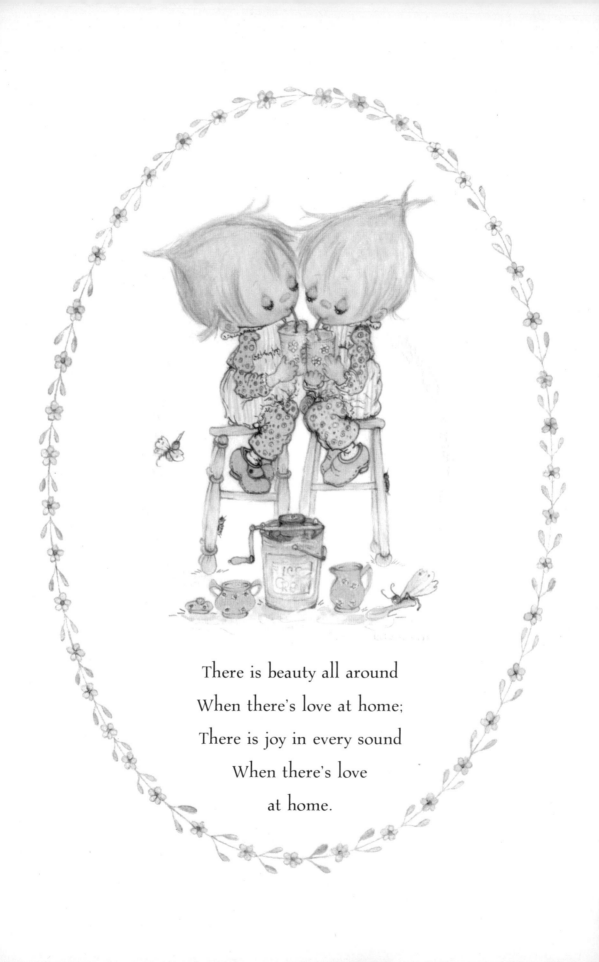

There is beauty all around
When there's love at home;
There is joy in every sound
When there's love
at home.

The Crown of the house
is Godliness.
The Beauty of the house is Order.
The Glory of the house
is Hospitality.
The Blessing of the house
is Contentment.

Say well and do well
End with one letter;
Say well is good,
Do well is better.

If a task is once begun,

Never leave it till it's done;

Be the labor great or small,

Do it well or not at all.

Do you count them only trifles?

What to earth are sun and rain?

Never was a kind word wasted;

Never was one said in vain.

One, two,

whatever you do,

Start it well,

and carry it through.

There is a time
for some things,
And a time for all things,
A time for great things,
And a time
for small things.

If your lips

you would keep from slips,

Five things observe with care:

Of whom you speak,

To whom you speak,

And how, and when, and where.

The world's a very happy place
where everyone
should dance and sing,
And always have a smiling face
and never sulk for anything.

How doth the little busy bee
Improve each shining hour
And gather honey all the day
From every passing flower!

They might not need me,
but they might.
I'll let my head
be just in sight;
A smile as small
as mine might be
Precisely their necessity.

Help us to do the things we should,

To be to others kind and good;

In all we do, in all we say,

To grow more loving

every day.

'Tis a lesson you should heed,

Try, try again;

If at first you don't succeed,

Try, try again.

Hearts, like doors,

will open with ease

To very, very little keys,

And don't forget

that two of these

Are "I thank you"

and "If you please."

Giving's receiving,
Receiving is giving!
That's really the secret
That lies behind living.

Whenever you're blue

find something to do

For somebody else

who is sadder

than you.

God wove a web of loveliness,
Of clouds and stars and birds,
But made not anything at all
So beautiful as words.

No one is too small
to be able to help a friend.

If you would reap praise,
You must sow the seeds:
Gentle words
And useful deeds.

Make new friends, but keep the old;
Those are silver, these are gold.

For every evil under the sun,

There is a remedy,

or there is none.

If there be one, try and find it;

If there be none,

never mind it.

There is so much bad
in the best of us
And so much good
in the worst of us,
That it doesn't behoove any of us
To talk about the rest of us.

Kind hearts are the gardens,
Kind words are the roots,
Kind thoughts are the flowers,
Kind deeds are the fruits...

...Take care of your garden
And keep out the weeds;
Fill it with sunshine,
Kind words
and good deeds.

Searching for stones,

I saw rough boulders;

Finding the thorn,

I missed the rose;

Looking for trouble,

I found a-plenty —

It's for us who seek it that trouble grows.

Searching for beauty,

I saw the morning!

Looking for joy,

I found no end;

Searching for peace,

I found the evening;

Trying to help, I gained a friend!

A true friend
is the best possession.

Time flies,

Suns rise

And shadows fall.

Let time go by.

Love is forever over all.

I love my friend
and the reason why
Is, "He is he and I am I."

I see the moon,
And the moon sees me;
God bless the moon,
And God bless me.

Willful waste makes woeful want,
And I may live to say,
Oh! How I wish I had the bread
That once I threw away!

I have upon my finger
A little piece of string,
To help me with some items
That need remembering.

Sometimes I wish I had one
Tied in a magic knot,
To help me with the matters
That need to be forgot.

Who has seen the wind?
Neither you nor I.
But when the trees
bow down their heads,
The wind is passing by.

If the sun and moon
should doubt,
They'd immediately go out.

Love the beautiful,
Seek out the true,
Wish for the good,
And the best do.

Life is mostly froth and bubble,

Two things stand like stone —

Kindness in another's trouble,

Courage in our own.

Just to be tender,
Just to be true,
Just to be glad
the whole day through,
Just to be cheery
when things go wrong...

...Just to drive sadness
away with a song,
Just to let love
be our daily key —
That is God's will
for you and me.

All things
bright and beautiful,
All creatures great and small,
All things wise and wonderful,
The Lord God made them all.

Back of the loaf is the snowy flour,

And back of the flour, the mill;

And back of the mill

is the wheat and the shower,

And the sun and the Father's will.

So here's my creed —
And how I love it!
Beauty in earth,
And God above it.

He who would live
in peace and at ease
Must not speak all he knows,
nor judge all he sees.

Of all the sayings in the world,
The one to see you through
Is "never trouble trouble
Till trouble troubles you."

So many gentle friends are near
Whom one can scarcely see,
I should never feel alone
Wherever I may be.

Solitude is very sad;
Too much company's
twice as bad.

This is wisdom, maids and men:
Knowing what to say
and when.

The world goes up
and the world goes down,
And the sunshine
follows the rain;
And yesterday's sneer
and yesterday's frown
Can never come back again.

Wealth is not his who has it,
But his who enjoys it.

There is nothing
either good or bad,
but thinking
makes it so.

Thank you, sun,
For your warmth and cheer.
Thank you, Lord,
For friends held dear.
Thank you, Father,
In heaven above —
For health, contentment,
Peace and love.

Composed
in the delicate and graceful Bernhard,
a twentieth-century typeface
designed by Lucian Bernhard of Germany.
Printed on
Hallmark Eggshell Book paper.
Designed by
Claudia Becker and Robert Haas.

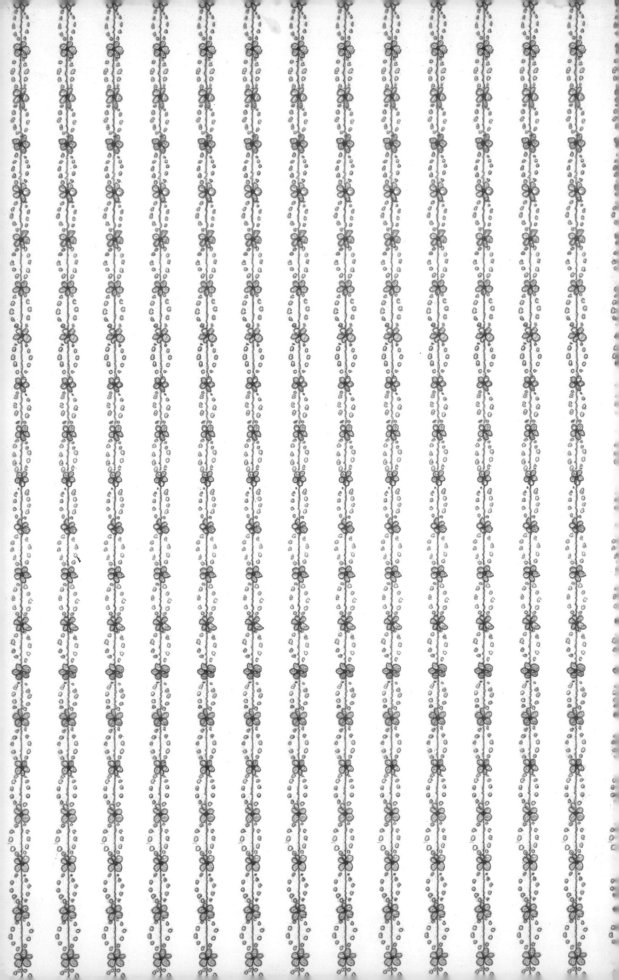